Gus and the Turkey

Story by Kris Bonnell

Pictures by David Wenzel

"Mmm, mmm,"
said Gus.
"Something smells good."

"Mom is cooking a turkey,"
Gus said to himself.
"The turkey smells so good."

"Mmm, mmm,"
Gus said to himself.
"The turkey looks good, too."

"Go away, Gus," said Mom. "I am not going to give you any turkey."

"The baby is eating turkey and green beans," said Gus. "Maybe the baby will drop some turkey."

11

"The baby dropped green beans," said Gus. "No turkey for me."